Tiling and Mosaics

in a weekend

Deena Beverley

MEREHURST

For Daisy. Thank you for demonstrating grout mixing and general apprentice skills, friendship and tolerance well in excess of your tender years.

Acknowledgements

As well as providing the photography that illustrates the finished projects, I would like to thank Andrew for his treatment of the step-by-step techniques photography. His practical approach has produced pictures that describe the making of the projects succinctly and enticingly.

I would also like to thank Anna Sanderson for giving me the opportunity to explore this subject in such a varied way, for her invaluable early contributions to the project concepts, and for her restrained, yet quietly encouraging, approach during the production of this book.

Heartfelt thanks to Karen Hemingway of Merehurst, with whom I first made the contact that led to the writing of this book, and who waited patiently as my working on it threatened to overwhelm all other projects in its path.

Finally, thank you to my husband and daughter for sharing my total immersion in this project with such good humour, enthusiasm and excessive reserves of stamina.

First published in 1999 by Merehurst Limited,
Ferry House, 51-57 Lacy Road, London SW15 1PR

Copyright © 1999 Merehurst Limited

ISBN 1 85391 738 9

A catalogue record for this book is available from the British Library.

Editor: Geraldine Christy
Designer: Sue Miller
Photographer: Andrew Newton-Cox
Stylist: Deena Beverley
Template illustrations: King & King
Commissioning Editor: Anna Sanderson
CEO & Publisher: Anne Wilson
International Sales Director: Mark Newman

Colour separation by Bright Arts, Hong Kong
Printed in Singapore by Tien Wah Press

Tiling and Mosaics

in a weekend

Contents

Introduction

Tiling and mosaics have enjoyed a massive resurgence of popularity in recent times. Certainly mosaic items and tile makeovers are amongst the most requested and well-received projects for home interest magazines and television programmes.

One of the most frequently asked questions is 'How can I cover up my hideous tiles?' That is why a high proportion of this book has been devoted to revamping existing tiled surfaces. The suggestions given are intended to be just that. Let your imagination run riot, and use the basic techniques and suggested materials as starting points to transform your own tile nightmares into exciting new decorating schemes.

Tile paints have improved dramatically in recent years. As long as you clean and condition the tiles thoroughly, following the manufacturer's directions absolutely to the letter, there is no reason why painted tiles will look second rate. As with most decorating projects, preparation, dull as it may be, is the key to success.

Also, consider the grout as being as important as the tiles in your makeover schemes. Although it is technically possible to clean grout and paint straight over it at the same time as the tiles, it can look horribly amateurish. It is advisable to steer clear of grout-renovating products that promise instant results. Follow the suggestion given in the Mediterranean colourwashed tile project, and rake out the surface of the old grout and start again. Tiles look best offset by fresh-looking, matt grout in a complementary colour.

The information given for grouting tiles applies equally to the mosaic projects as to the tile projects. After all, mosaic projects are just tiling projects using smaller tiles. To clear up any confusion you may have regarding the difference between the words tiles and tesserae – there isn't any! Tesserae has become a generally accepted term used to describe the individual components of any mosaic.

Now that mosaic is so popular, many shops are selling mosaic supplies, but may be uninformed about their applications. In contrast, specialist mosaic suppliers, however friendly, can be somewhat baffling with their in-depth knowledge of their craft. To ease your learning curve, here is all you need to know about mosaic in a nutshell. There are two basic mosaic working methods: direct and indirect.

Direct is where tesserae are applied directly onto a surface. It is the simplest, most satisfyingly immediate way to work, and is used throughout this book.

Indirect refers to the method where tesserae are applied to a backing sheet, then inverted onto a surface. This enables mosaicists to work away from the site, for example when working on a large, exterior project. Another application of the indirect method is when an absolutely flat surface is required, but the precise uniformity of the results can be disappointingly soulless.

For the direct working method used here, apply tesserae rippled side down. Ceramic, vitreous and metallic tesserae are essentially all the same thing: small, flat machine-made square tiles that are generally halved and quartered with nippers. The colours and texture are what differentiates them. Smalti are hand-made tiles that are often used in the self-grouting method; that is, just pushed into adhesive or grout, which then rises up to surround each one.

Mosaic is a medium that is infinitely variable according to your own tastes and the amount of time and effort you wish to expend. These projects should give you a taste of the exciting possibilities afforded by this most immediate and satisfying of crafts.

Deena Beverley

Mediterranean colourwashed tiles

Your existing plain machine-made tiles can attain an expensive-looking hand-painted finish. Bring a touch of Mediterranean rusticity to them with a simple colourwashed effect.

Planning your time

DAY ONE
AM: Rake out old grout; clean and condition tiles; paint on first coat of glaze to all tiles

PM: Paint on subsequent coats of glaze; varnish

DAY TWO
AM: Grout

Tools and materials

Grout-removing tool

Ceramic paints, cleaner/conditioner, glaze and varnish (from same range for best compatibility)

Paintbrushes

Powdered grout, natural buff colour

Kitchen paper

Clean rags

Wooden tongue depressor

Disposable mixing bowls for grout (for example, cleaned-out food containers)

Tile squeegee

Tin foil

Tile or old plate to use as palette

This tiled wall suffered from two problems. First, the undulating surface, in a room with little natural light, looked permanently dingy – white without light on it merely looks grey! Second, the grout had seen better days, and was unappealingly grubby, with or without the effects of light.

Hand-made and painted Mediterranean tiles are universally admired for their rich, glowing tones and depth of colour. Choose a warm palette of closely related subtle earth shades to produce a folksy, homely look.

Now the light hitting the ripples in the tiles has something to play with, and reveals the many layers of colour built up by repeated colourwashing. Each layer is a shade slightly different to the one beneath which gives added interest to the surface.

This technique could be applied to any tile, not just white. However, it would be a good idea to blank out any really hideously distracting colour in white, or better still, ivory-coloured tile paint before you begin building up your beautiful translucent glazes. They would not look nearly as effective on a turquoise or avocado base!

Although coloured grout is available, the colour palette available at present is so restricted that it is well worth making your own by simply colouring the water with which the powder grout is mixed by using universal stainers or acrylic paint.

Day One

Step 1

Rake out old grout with grout-removing tool.

Step 2

Thoroughly clean and condition the tiles using a product from the same range as the paints. Follow the manufacturer's directions precisely for best results.

Step 3

On a foil-covered plate or tile, dilute ceramic paint with the glaze so that it produces a translucent coloured mixture. Using foil enables you to change the colour frequently without needing to stop and clean the palette each time.

Step 4

Paint on the glaze with a brush to leave deliberate brush marks in one direction only. Continue to paint the tiles to produce a random effect. Leave one or two in their original colours. Vary the direction of the brush marks from tile to tile for an authentic, handcrafted appearance to the walls.

Step 5

Mix small quantities of additional coloured glaze to produce closely related toning shades. Brush these on top of the colours when the first colour is dry. Leave to dry.

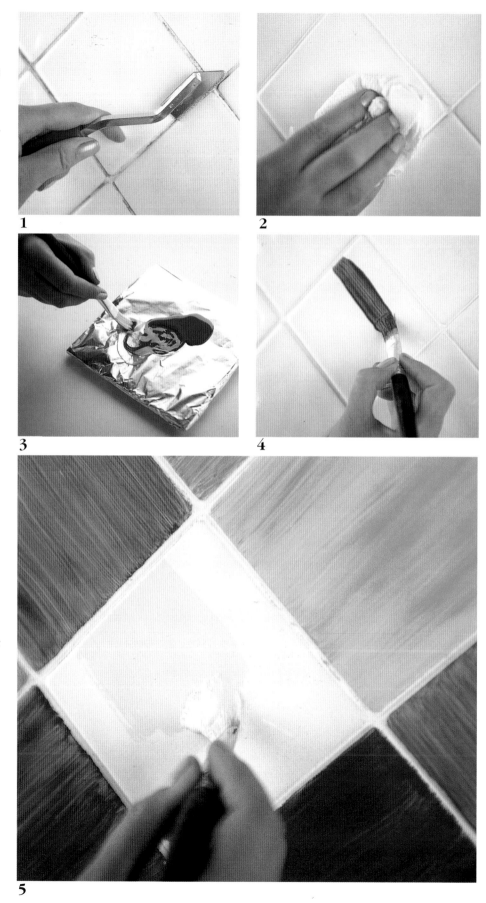

6

8

7

Step 6
Add several coats of varnish, allowing each coat to dry thoroughly before applying the next. Leave to set fully overnight.

Day Two

Step 7
Colour water with red and burnt umber universal stainers or acrylic paint. Add PVA adhesive in a ratio of approximately 1 part PVA to 5 parts water. Use this to make up the powder grout to a dryish, mud-pie consistency.

Step 8
Apply grout with a tile squeegee and spread evenly, taking care to push it well down into the gaps between the tiles. Remove excess gently with a soft rag. Allow to dry thoroughly.

Pebble mosaic floor

Interspersing terracotta tiles with pebble mosaic makes an unusual decorative patio feature. This project would also make a charming floor surface for a summerhouse or conservatory.

Most gardens have an area that could use a little hard flooring, but concrete slabs are just too awful to contemplate. Specialist hand-made exterior flooring surfaces look great, but can prove expensive over a large area. This pebble mosaic solution borrows from an age-old tradition of using pebbles for abstract and pictorial effects. The result is inexpensive, surprisingly simple to achieve, and looks equally at home in town or country gardens.

It is important to prepare the groundwork well before you begin. Although you want a striking textural finish, aim to have the tops of the pebbles exactly level with the surface of the tiles so that the floor is even and comfortable to walk on. You do not want a surface that causes garden furniture to wobble irritatingly, so take care to level the dry mix before you place the pebbles within it, and take equal care to push all the pebbles in to leave a uniform height.

Contrary to what seems a natural way of working, the pebbles in pebble mosaic are not simply laid lengthwise on the surface of the dry mix, but are pushed down into it end on, for maximum strength. As you work, you will quickly become accustomed to selecting pebbles for their size and appearance when viewed end on.

Please do not take pebbles from beaches without checking with the local authority. Legitimately collected pebbles, conveniently graded according to size, are available inexpensively from specialist suppliers, who can often deliver heavy loads and provide invaluable advice and help with preparing your individual base prior to commencing the decorative part of the work. If you have an existing unsightly paved area you could also consider removing alternate slabs, and filling in the gaps with pebble mosaic.

Day One

Step 1

Prepare a concrete base 5-7.5 cm (2-3 in) thick to give a flat surface 10 cm (4 in) below what will become the finished ground level. Leave to dry overnight, covered with damp sacking to prevent too rapid curing during dry weather, or add dry sacking/plastic sheeting to protect against frost in winter if you live in a cold climate.

Day Two

Step 2

Prepare mortar 'dry mix'. Mix three parts of sharp sand to one part of cement - leave dry, do not add water.

Step 3

Pour dry mix onto concrete base and smooth flat using a straightedge until the mix is lower than the finished ground level by the thickness of the tiles.

Step 4

Construct the main pebble motif by pushing pebbles end on into the dry mix so that they protrude by the thickness of the tiles. Make sure the height is uniform.

Step 5

Bed terracotta tiles onto the dry mix using a slight wiggling motion for good adhesion.

Ready-made 'dry mix'

It is possible to buy bags of aggregate and cement which contain the right proportions of each, individually bagged within one sack; this saves you the bother of having to calculate ratios.

1

2

3

4

5

6

7

8

Step 6

Place further pebbles to fill in the rest of the design.

Step 7

Brush dry mix evenly over the surface to fill any gaps, then sprinkle the whole area with water. The dry mix will absorb the water and begin to set hard over the following few days.

Step 8

Cover with sacking or plastic sheeting supported clear of the mosaic surface by a board until the mortar has completely cured (about a week). Avoid walking on the area if possible for three weeks or so.

Painted fabric tiles

Give your kitchen tiles a more homely look with painted patchwork motifs. Copy scraps of fabric from elsewhere in your decorating scheme for a co-ordinated look.

Plain large-sized tiles are a popular and practical choice for kitchens, but large areas of them can look clinical and cold. Hand-painting existing tiles that are sound, but uninspiring, sometimes seems daunting, but this project utilizes a stamping technique to produce neat, infinitely repeatable results in record time. A few deft brushstrokes to highlight the floral elements of the design gives a laboriously hand-painted feel without actually being labour intensive.

This design takes the colourful painterly fabric of the curtains as its inspiration, but you could restrict yourself to any one of the stamping techniques shown in the instructions for an equally effective result. The gingham motif in particular, would work well scaled up onto a bigger stamp for even faster results.

Whatever you decide, do not skip the initial stage of painting brushstrokes in a colour that is almost the same as the colour of the tile. The process may seem boring, but the slight difference in tone beneath the stamped motifs is what gives an overall warm effect of painted fabric rather than cold, glazed tile. The naive, open pattern created by the sponge also looks more comfortable over a broken-colour ground than on harsh white.

If you are using this project to revamp existing tiles that are not an obliging white or ivory, simply blank out their colour with neutral-coloured tile primer and tile paint before you begin to add the patterns.

Planning your time

DAY ONE

AM: Clean and condition tiles; mask grout and surrounding area. Apply ground colour; mark out patchwork 'pieces'. Cut out sponge shapes; stamp on. Apply polka dots

PM: Cut out sponge gingham shapes; apply gingham and checked motifs. Add leaf and flower detail

DAY TWO

AM: Add 'stitch lines'; remove pencil marks

PM: Varnish; remove masking tape

Tools and materials

Cold set ceramic paints, cleaner/conditioner and satin varnish (from same range for best compatibility)

Flat, stiff paintbrush

Fine paintbrush

Lighter fuel

Tin foil

Tile or old plate for palette

Expandable sponge (from craft shops)

Quilting tape (narrow masking tape sold in quilting shops)

Masking tape

Ballpoint pen

Cotton buds

Cocktail sticks

Small scissors

Ruler

Pencil

Thin card

Ceramic outliner in dark colour to tone with colour scheme

Day One

Step 1
Prepare tiles using cleaner and conditioner, following the manufacturer's directions precisely.

Step 2
Mask off grout with quilting tape to preserve the visual contrast between the matt grout and the slight sheen of the finished tiles. (If you want a really speedy result, simply omit this stage and brush over the entire surface, grout and all.) Mask off surrounding area with standard-width masking tape to protect against overpainting.

Step 3
Brush cream-coloured paint over the tiles, leaving deliberate brush marks in one direction only. Allow the base colour of the tile to show through.

Step 4
Using a ruler and pencil, lightly mark out the tiles into smaller rectangles and triangles to mimic patchwork pieces.

Step 5
Draw simple leaf and flower shapes onto an expandable sponge with a ball-point pen. Cut out using small scissors. Place the shapes in water so that the sponge expands.

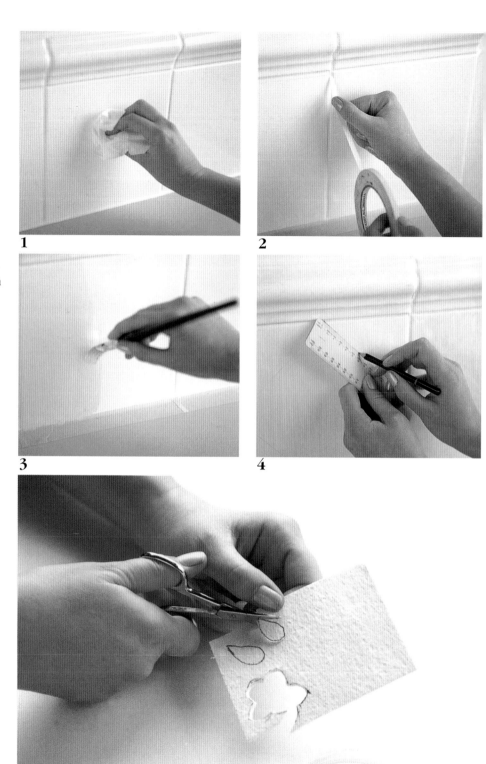

6

Step 6

Dab the sponge flower shape onto a foil-covered plate or tile to pick up a minimal amount of ceramic paint. Holding a card to shield the marked-off edge of a patchwork 'piece', stamp flower motifs onto a random number of patchwork 'pieces'.

Step 7

Apply leaf motifs in the same way. Make sure that the motifs 'break' the edge of the patchwork pieces visually for a realistic printed fabric effect.

7

Using stiff-bristled brushes

Really cheap, stiff brushes are perfect for some of the brush painting in this project, which actually requires visible brush marks that allow the base colour to show through. Their stiffness also means that they pick up and hold very little paint, making it easy to apply just a thin coat.

Step 8

Using a sliver of sponge, bend it between your fingers as you stamp on the flower stems, to produce natural-looking curves.

Step 9

Dip a cotton bud into a small amount of paint to produce polka dots. As with the flowers and leaves, apply dots that seem to disappear between the 'seams' of the patchwork pieces for a fabric-like effect.

Step 10

Cut small squares from the expandable sponge. Insert a cocktail stick into the sponge to form a handle. To form the gingham motif, paint rows of squares, leaving a gap roughly the same size as the piece of sponge between each one.

Step 11

Mix a colour which is 50 per cent lighter in tone to the first colour of the gingham design. Stamp in between the rows of existing squares to complete the motif.

Step 12

Using a barely loaded, stiff-bristled flat brush, paint a loose, checked design onto some of the remaining 'pieces'.

Using coloured grout

For a really vibrant look replace dingy grout with brightly coloured grouting before starting to decorate the tiles. Just add colour to the mixing water with universal stainers or acrylic paint.

8

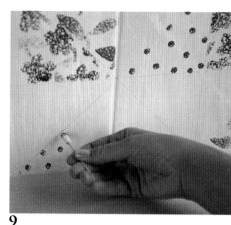

9

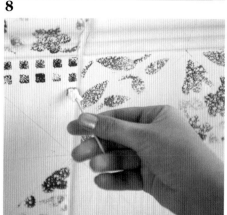

10

11

12

13

15

Step 13

Using a fine paintbrush, add a few lines of toning, darker colour to the flower and leaf motifs for added visual emphasis. Keep the lines free and spontaneous.

Day Two

Step 14

Using a ceramic outliner in a dark, toning colour, paint on 'stitch lines' close to the edge of some of the tiles to mimic running stitch, cross stitch and oversewing. Allow to dry thoroughly. Remove any visible pencil lines with lighter fuel on a cotton bud, using a gentle sweeping motion.

Step 15

Apply several coats of satin finish ceramic varnish, allowing each coat to dry thoroughly before applying the next. Remove the masking tape.

14

Gingham bath panel

Freshen up your bathroom with this crisp gingham-influenced design for a bath panel. It utilizes reject tiles and is a satisfyingly fast-growing project.

Planning your time

DAY ONE
AM: Plan design; mark out bath panel; cut tiles

PM: Clean, scuff and seal bath panel. Apply white tiles. Apply border tiles

DAY TWO
AM: Grout

Tools and materials

Tile cutter

Tiles – white, light blue, dark blue

White waterproof tile adhesive

Buff-coloured grout powder

Goggles

Gloves

Notched spreader

Scuffing tool

PVA

Brush for applying PVA

Tile nippers

Tape measure

Pencil

Straightedge

Rags for grouting

Coloured pencils

Squared paper

Bath panels are generally not seen as the most exciting aspect of a bathroom scheme, which can be a mistake. This fresh gingham design can easily be translated into any coloured check to suit your own décor and will definitely create an impact. The only point to remember when choosing colours is to make the paler tone roughly 50 per cent lighter than the darker tone. If the difference in tone is too great, the fabric feel will be lost. Here a blue chambray coloured tile with a speckled texture and matt finish has been used to give a cottony feel, which works well with dark

blue. Most machine-made coloured tiles are available in a matt finish as well as the more usual gloss. Ask your tile supplier for details.

Larger tiles are used for the bulk of the panel. The remaining, checked design makes canny use of a tile cutter to transform a few boxes of standard plain-coloured reject tiles into homemade tesserae.

Cutting the rounded edges off all the tiles gives them a crisp square edge and an authentic mosaic look. However, you could simply apply uncut plain white tiles to the main part of the panel and finish with a single border of the checkerboard design if you want a speedier result.

Here a buff-coloured grout replaces the usual white. It is every bit as important to consider grout colour carefully as to choose tile colour. The grout delineates the tiles and should serve to emphasize their colour and placement. White grout tends to dominate visually and somehow leeches colour from the surrounding tiles. The natural colour here also picks up on the styling of the room, which has a Shaker feel, and prevents the mosaic from looking too cold and clinical. Use spare tiles to trim mirrors and other accessories to match.

Day One

Step 1
Experiment with the design on paper until you achieve a design that will work both visually and physically for the size of the panel; remember to allow for grout widths in all your calculations.

Step 2
Measure and mark out the design onto the bath panel, dividing the dimensions to give the sizes to which the tiles will need to be cut.

Step 3
Cut large squares of white tile to size using a tile cutter. Cut border tiles into strips ready for nipping into smaller squares.

Step 4
Wearing goggles and gloves, use nippers to cut the border tile strips into squares and place each different colour into a separate container.

Step 5
Clean, then scuff, the bath panel to provide a key for the tile adhesive.

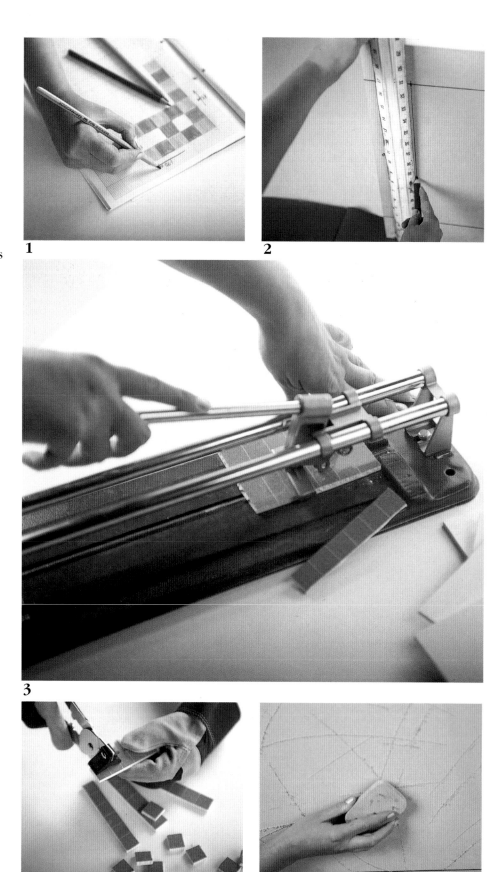

1

2

3

4

5

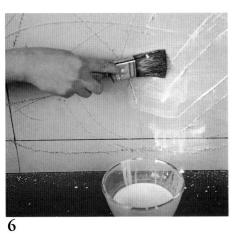

6

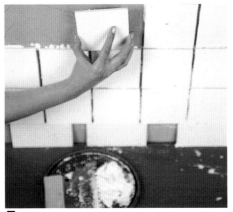

7

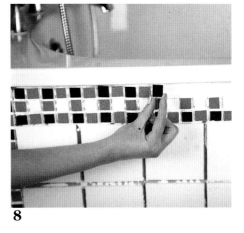

8

9

Step 6

Seal the scuffed surface with PVA glue diluted 50/50 with water.

Step 7

Apply tile adhesive to the reverse of the large white tiles using a notched spreader and press into place using a slight twisting motion. Use offcuts of white tile trimmed to the border width to support the tiles while the adhesive starts to set.

Step 8

Apply tile adhesive to the border area a little at a time and press in the trimmed tesserae in the correct order to form the pattern you worked out in Step 1. Leave to set overnight.

Day Two

Step 9

Mix waterproof buff tile grout with water that has had waterproof PVA added in a ratio of roughly 1 part PVA to 5 parts water. With a sponge or rags, and with the grout mixed fairly dry and stiff, work the grout into the joints using a circular motion. Polish any grout from the face of the tiles with a clean rag to finish.

Alternative checks

For an even faster project, tile the main part of the panel with white tiles and finish with a border of tiles printed or painted in a gingham design.

Garden tool store

Store all those bits and pieces of garden paraphernalia that otherwise seem to end up on the floor of the garden shed in this quirkily decorative cupboard.

An old wall-mounted cupboard is transformed into a useful garden storage area; perhaps for all those smaller, fiddly items such as secateurs and plant ties that seem to become easily displaced in the average crowded shed.

Many of us find old garden tools quite irresistible. This project utilizes inexpensive junk-shop finds in this charming mosaic of found objects, which also includes the rim and base sections of tiny terracotta pots.

Grouting such a myriad collection of shapes and sizes is painstaking work, involving almost the meticulous care involved in an archeological dig. As you rub away the grout to reveal the keys and tile shards lurking beneath you must be careful not to take the level of the grout down so far as to reveal the tile adhesive, yet you need to uncover every lovingly applied mosaic piece.

By using a combined tile adhesive/grout product applied thickly, and simply pushing the pieces into place, the project could effectively be completed as the mosaic is constructed, without the need for separate grouting. However, a separately applied grout unifies and smooths the delineations between the mosaic pieces so pleasingly that the more labour-intensive option is recommended without hesitation.

Planning your time

DAY ONE
AM: Cut bases off pots. Plan design. Scuff and seal cupboard front. Nip pot shards and rims into smaller pieces

PM: Apply adhesive to cupboard front and apply mosaic

DAY TWO
AM: Grout; remove excess with abrasive pad

Tools and materials

Wall-mounted cupboard with recessed door

Old terracotta pots

Tile saw

Miniature terracotta pots (from floristry supplier)

Old keys

Old hand fork

Scuffing tool

Waterproof PVA adhesive

Paintbrush

Pebbles

Abrasive kitchen pads

Dark grey frost-proof powdered grout

Waterproof tile adhesive

Tile nippers

Clean rags

Disposable gloves

Patio cleaner (from tile shops) or dilute hydrochloric acid (from chemists)

Dust mask

Goggles

Adhesive spreader

Short-bristled hard stencil brush

Day One

Step 1
Cut bases from terracotta pots using a tile saw. Wear goggles and a dust mask to avoid breathing in fine particles and work in a well-ventilated area.

Step 2
Experiment with your design on the cupboard front and lay it out roughly on paper alongside.

Step 3
Scuff the surface of the cupboard front with a scuffing tool. Seal it with PVA adhesive diluted roughly 1 part PVA to 5 parts water.

Step 4
Spread adhesive evenly over the door recess. Embed the fork in the adhesive.

Step 5
Add pot bases and keys to build up a symmetrical pattern.

Cleaning mosaic thoroughly

Really bring out the sparkle in the keys and fork, and remove residual grout film by cleaning the entire mosaic a few days after finishing it. Use patio cleaner or dilute hydrochloric acid. Wear protective gloves and goggles, and rinse the mosaic liberally with water afterwards. Polish with a clean, dry rag.

1

2

3

4

5

8

6

7

Step 6
Wearing goggles, nip terracotta pot rims into small, narrow lengths and insert them into the adhesive to form a border. Use large sections to make smooth corners.

Step 7
Fill in the gaps with broken pot fragments, small pots and pebbles. Nip smashed pot fragments into even smaller pieces if necessary using nippers. Build up the design more or less symmetrically, but allow the work to remain quite free, with different sizes and shapes of fragment giving a spontaneous, fresh feel. Leave to set overnight.

Day Two

Step 8
Mix up powder grout using water in which PVA has been diluted in a ratio of approximately 1 part PVA to 5 parts water. Make the grout fairly stiff and dry. Wearing protective gloves, remove excess grout by scrubbing with an abrasive kitchen pad and short-bristled hard stencil brush until all the mosaic elements are uncovered.

Découpage floral tiles

Découpage, that pastime so beloved of Victorian ladies, is updated in this fresh-as-a-daisy makeover for unattractive tiles. The motifs are simply cut from giftwrap.

A frequently asked question is how to revamp unsightly tiles that would be expensive to replace and very time-consuming to do. Acres of horrible tiles evidently cover the globe!

This project was devised with this in mind and it incorporates both applied decoration in the form of découpage and a paint treatment that does not look 'home-made'. Even viewed in unforgiving close-up, the tiles look as if they were purchased with this lively floral design on a vivid painterly ground.

The key to producing a similarly convincing result is to take care to match the painted background exactly to the giftwrap, so that the floral motif appears fully integrated with the ground colour. Découpage was originally devised to mimic expensively hand-painted items; so you are continuing an age-old craft tradition by blending the cut-out shape with the background in this way. Use good quality giftwrap for a smooth finish.

The simple outlines of the flowers make the cutting out easy to do. If you are embarking on this project as an emergency makeover for really awful coloured tiles, blank out the offending shade with tile primer and white tile paint before adding the sponged colour and découpage motifs.

Planning your time

DAY ONE
AM: Clean, mask off and condition tiles; sponge on base colour

PM: Sponge on second colour. Cut out floral motifs; glue in place; allow to dry overnight

DAY TWO
AM: Remove masking tape. Varnish

PM: Add subsequent coats of varnish, allowing each to dry thoroughly before applying the next

Tools and materials

Giftwrap with floral motifs

Nail scissors

Cold set ceramic paints, varnish and cleaner/conditioner (from same range for best compatibility)

Waterproof PVA adhesive

Masking tape

Palette

Disposable gloves

Paintbrush

Kitchen paper

Scalpel

Day One

Step 1
Clean tiles thoroughly.

Step 2
Using masking tape, mask off tiles that are to remain plain.

Step 3
Apply proprietary tile conditioner to tiles that are to be painted. Follow the manufacturer's directions precisely.

Step 4
Sponge the paler, base colour evenly over the tile, allowing some of the white tile to show through. Use only a tiny amount of paint on the sponge. The paint will dry almost immediately since the amount used is so minimal.

Step 5
Sponge the darker colour on top of the lighter base. Allow to dry completely before applying flower motifs.

1

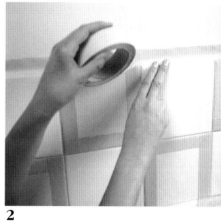

2

3

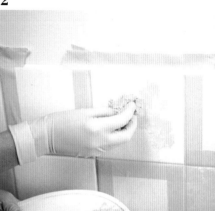

4

5

Choosing varnish

Matt varnish has been used here to provide a pleasing contrast with the shiny white tiles; but you may prefer a satin, or high gloss finish, depending on the surface of the surrounding tiles. The more coats you apply, the more resilient and cohesive the result.

6

8

Step 6
Cut motifs from giftwrap using nail scissors. Take care to remove all the background colour from around the cut-out motif.

Step 7
Using PVA diluted with water in a roughly 1:1 ratio, glue the flower motifs centrally on top of the sponged tiles. Smooth out any air bubbles as the glue dries. If any large pockets of air form between parts of the paper and the tile, simply puncture these with a scalpel and they will flatten.

Day Two

Step 8
Remove the masking tape. Apply several coats of matt varnish, allowing each coat to dry thoroughly before applying the next.

7

White and silver crazy mosaic pots

Inexpensive machine-made terracotta pots attain designer status with a sprinkling of silver tesserae and a coating of smart white tiles, adding a touch of glamour to your planting.

C ontainer gardening is always popular. Plants can be moved around to suit the seasons and to give an ever-changing display both in and out of the house. However, one problem with growing plants in containers is that the plants keep growing! It sometimes seems that no sooner has a plant been repotted than it grows enthusiastically out of its new container. Keeping up can become quite expensive, particularly as some plants achieve substantial sizes. Machine-made terracotta pots are an affordable solution but they are are not always inspiring to look at.

The simplest ideas are often the most effective. Here, inexpensive reject tiles in classic white have been smashed into random fragments and applied to pots interspersed with bands of sparkling silvery mirrored tesserae. Using waterproof adhesive and grout, and taking care to seal the porous surface of the pot before starting to mosaic, they are as robust as they are striking.

Suitable for conservatory or garden applications, these pots can be left outside even in colder weather. If you live in a cold climate, make sure you use frost-proof grout. When the summer marguerites have faded, they can be replaced with evergreen topiary spheres whose architectural shape will complement the pots.

A few days after completion, when the grout has set hard, you may like to give the mosaic an additional clean with hydrochloric acid (available from chemists) or patio cleaner. This gives the finished pots an unbeatable sparkle. Wear gloves and goggles and work in a well-ventilated area. After cleaning, rinse the pots liberally with water before drying with a soft cloth.

Day One

Step 1

If pots are for exterior use, and are not frost proof, seal inside and out by brushing on waterproof PVA adhesive diluted with water in a ratio of approximately 1:1.

Step 2

Place a few mirrored tesserae on the pot to assess the width of the band or spiral you require. Remember to allow enough space for grout between each tessera and between the edge of the band and the rest of the mosaic. Using masking tape, draw the position of the design roughly with pencil or chalk.

Step 3

Wearing goggles and gloves, roughly break the white tiles using a hammer, by wrapping them individually in sacking and tapping sharply at the centre. Open the sacking to check that the tile is sufficiently broken. Close the sacking and repeat until pieces are the desired size.

Step 4

Wearing gloves to protect your hands, apply tiles around the border of the pot, using waterproof EVA glue or waterproof PVA. For a professional, finished look, place the glazed, rounded-off edge of the tile next to the border.

Step 5

Wearing goggles and gloves, use nippers to break tiles further if necessary to fit. Hold the nippers with the curved side against the tile, just in from the edge and snap cleanly. Glue on pieces of white tile to cover all parts of the pot apart from what will be the mirrored band and the top of the rim. Continue the white tiles down inside the pot to approximately the point that will become the soil fill level. This gives a solid look to the finished pot. Keep the gaps between the pieces even.

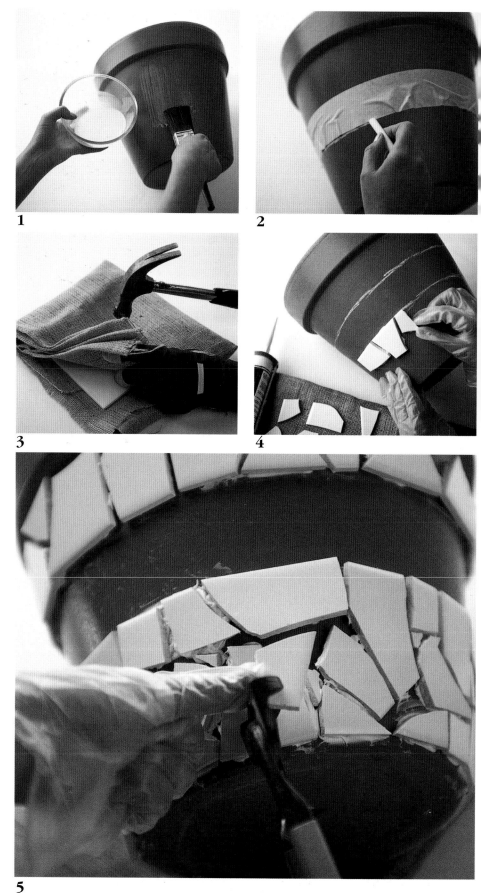

6

7

8

9

Step 6
Cut lengths of white tile on a tile cutter, to a width that will sit neatly across the top of the pot rim, spanning the thickness of the rim and the tiles already applied to the interior and exterior of the pot.

Step 7
Nip the long strips into smaller pieces, roughly square, and glue on with EVA or waterproof PVA to cover the rim of the pot. Do not worry about calculating the circumference and dividing it equally by the amount of tiles. Simply adjust the gap between each tile minutely as you complete the rim mosaic. The eye will absorb any tiny adjustment and read the rim tiles as being evenly spaced.

Step 8
Since the mirrored tesserae are much thinner than the white tiles, you will need to build up quite a thick layer of EVA adhesive or waterproof PVA before applying the defining spiral or bands of mirrored tile in order to keep them level with the surface of the white tiles. When you have finished, leave to set overnight.

Day Two

Step 9
Mix frost-proof grey grout with water that has had waterproof PVA added in a ratio of approximately 1 part PVA to 5 parts water. Aim for a dryish, mud-pie consistency. Wearing gloves, apply the grout to the mosaic, taking care to push it well into all the gaps. Rub away excess grout with a dry rag.

Making mosaic tiles

As well as being the most affordable option, machine-made tiles are the ideal choice for mosaic projects; they are thinner than their more expensive, hand-made counterparts and therefore smash and nip very easily. Most tile shops have a selection of seconds, or visit a factory shop for affordable inspiration.

China patchwork doorstep

A neglected, age-worn doorstep becomes a real show stopper bedecked in irresistibly pretty broken china. Patterned saucers add interest and colour to the front of the step.

The doorstep is generally ignored as an opportunity for applied decoration. However, since it is one of the first details visitors see as they approach your home, it is worth spending a little effort to make it into a real focal point that will lift the spirits.

Many of us are inveterate purchasers and hoarders of mismatched china – particularly pretty saucers, which are usually inexpensive at boot sales, junk shops and markets. However, there is a limit to the number of plates and saucers that you can hang on the walls without making your home look like a pub or an 'olde worlde tea shoppe'. This project justifies your china shopping expeditions admirably.

Small saucers decorate the vertical front of the step, sized to suit the step. An old dollies teaset would yield adorable tiny china plates and saucers for a shallow step. The gaps between the saucers are filled with broken china fragments, predominantly in white so as to focus attention on the saucers themselves. The gaps could equally be filled with broken tiles.

On the horizontal surface of the step, the saucer motif is picked up by replicating their round shapes in mosaic, using sections of flat plate rims to define each roundel while producing a hard-wearing, practical flat surface. Again, the gaps are filled with china and tile fragments.

Planning your time

DAY ONE
AM: Scuff step. 'Fit' saucers to front of step; fix saucers; apply thick bed of adhesive; leave to dry

PM: Smash/nip china and apply to fill in gaps between saucers. Apply roundels to top of step. Leave to set overnight

DAY TWO
AM: Grout

Tools and materials

Saucers

Plates with pretty rims

Plates with pretty centres

White china

Patio cleaner (from tile shops) or dilute hydrochloric acid (from chemists)

Scrap china or discarded tesserae

Tile nippers

Gloves

Goggles

Scuffing tool

Waterproof PVA adhesive

Chalk

Abrasive kitchen pads

Stiff, short-bristled stencil brush

Hammer

Sacking

Adhesive spreader

Wooden tongue depressors

Waterproof tile adhesive (grey)

Day One

Step 1
Scuff the surface of the step and seal with PVA adhesive that is diluted approximately 1 part PVA to 5 parts water.

Step 2
Trial fit the saucers to the front surface of the step. Mark out their positions with chalk.

Step 3
Liberally spread tile adhesive onto the rear of each saucer and to the front of the step just inside the circled area that marks the saucer position. Apply the saucer to the front of the step.

Step 4
Fill in the area around the saucers with a thick bed of adhesive, making sure that it completely fills the area beneath the sloped underside of each saucer. Build up the depth of adhesive until it is almost level with the saucer rims. You are aiming to give the impression that the saucers are embedded within a solid step rather than having been applied to the surface, as well as providing a strong, solid surface that will withstand pedestrian traffic. Leave to dry.

Step 5
Wearing gloves and goggles, wrap the china in folded sacking and smash it with a hammer into pieces. Then nip predominantly white china into smaller, triangular pieces. Smash and nip coloured and patterned plate rims to make circular motifs on top of the step.

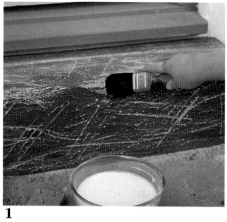

1

2

3

4

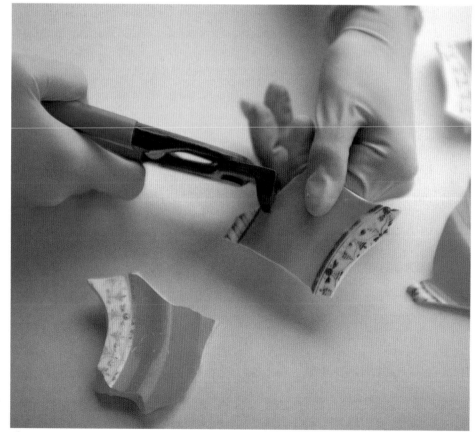

5

6

7

8

9

Step 6

Apply white triangular fragments to fill the gaps on the front of the step. Prop up lower triangles if necessary with scraps of china or discarded tesserae.

Step 7

'Butter' individual fragments and apply them to build up a roundel design on the horizontal surface of the step. Take great care to embed the china evenly. Since the china is probably of varying thickness, you will need to push thick pieces well down into the adhesive, and build up adhesive thickly behind thinner pieces to bring them up to the same level. Aim to produce as flat a surface as possible.

Step 8

Fill in areas around the roundels with white fragments. Leave to dry overnight.

Day Two

Step 9

Mix PVA into water in a ratio of approximately 1 part PVA to 5 parts water. Use this water to mix the grout to a dryish, mud-pie consistency. Wearing protective gloves, spread the grout liberally over the mosaic, working in one area at a time.

Step 10

Push the grout well into the gaps. Remove the excess as you work with a dry cloth and abrasive kitchen pads. Remove tricky bits of grout with a stiff-bristled stencil brush. Give the mosaic another final clean a couple of days after completing, with patio cleaner or dilute hydrochloric acid to bring out the full sparkle of the mosaic. Wear goggles and gloves during handling. Rinse the step thoroughly afterwards with clean water and polish with a soft cloth.

10

Playing card mosaic splashback

This intricate-looking mosaic effect, created from just a few playing cards, gives new life to old tiles. This project opens endless possibilities since so many designs are available.

P laying cards are ideally suited to many applications where tiles are commonly used. They are already sealed with a durable plastic finish, and their crisp, geometric designs lend themselves readily to reproducing seemingly complex mosaic effects at minimal cost and effort.

The cobalt blue colourway used here is a perennial winner for bathroom schemes, and it is easy to find similar playing cards to these ones in high street stationers and toy shops.

Junk shops also can yield an interesting selection of inexpensive old playing cards with richly textural

designs on the reverse. Many of these sets of cards are incomplete and of no use to card players. Even if the cards have been much handled, by peeling away the layers of the playing card to leave only the patterned, uppermost layer, you are left with a thin, strong, coated paper that is perfectly clean and usefully slightly raised on the side that needs to stick to the tile. This laborious, but critical, step also means that fewer layers of varnish need to be added once the mosaic is assembled in order to achieve a flat, hard-wearing surface. The more layers of varnish you add, the more professional it will look.

If the intricate placing of the tiny components seems like an unbearably fiddly task, simply apply the patterns more or less whole, without breaking them down into smaller parts. The effect may not have quite such a mosaic-type look, but will still be very striking.

Planning your time

DAY ONE
AM: Clean tiles. Experiment with design. Peel off card fronts; cut card fronts into smaller units. Apply outer border

PM: Mark out grid. Apply internal border and squares. Apply tiny squares at the intersection of each inner border

DAY TWO
AM: Paint diluted PVA over tiles; leave to dry. Varnish; leave to dry

PM: Paint on subsequent coats of varnish

Tools and materials

Pack of playing cards

Waterproof PVA adhesive

Glass cleaner

Kitchen paper

Small paintbrush

Acrylic varnish

Pencil

Ruler

Graph paper

Small scissors

Cotton buds

Cocktail stick

Overhead projector marker pen

Day One

Step 1

Clean tiles thoroughly with glass cleaner to remove any hint of grease.

Step 2

Cut up some card reverses into smaller units and borders. Experiment with your design. Calculate and roughly draw out how many smaller units are necessary to produce the nine blocks in this design, depending on the size of tiles you are decorating.

Step 3

Peel the reverse of the playing cards away from the fronts so that you are left with one thin layer of coated paper.

Step 4

Cut the thinned card reverse into smaller components as needed for your design – for example, blocks of four flower motifs, single motifs, and lengths of borders.

Step 5

Mix waterproof PVA adhesive with water in a ratio of approximately 1:1. Glue the outer borders. Be careful not to glue layers of paper on top of each other at the corners as this will produce too much bulk. Instead, overlap the layers, then trim the join neatly and cleanly with a scalpel.

1

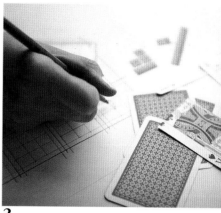

2

3

4

5

Making it last

Although hard wearing and wipe clean-able, this project, like all those involving applied layers, is not ideally suited to applications where it would be required to withstand a constant onslaught of water, such as shower surrounds.

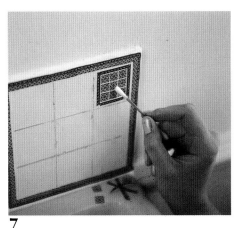

5

7

Step 6

Using an overhead projection marker pen, mark out the tile into a grid forming nine squares.

Step 7

Spread dilute PVA glue over one of the smaller squares formed by the grid. Apply a narrow border in a square within this. Fill this square with small blocks, evenly spaced. Make any adjustments to placing by using a cotton bud to ease the small component parts of the design gently into place.

Step 8

Finish off each corner of the newly formed square border with a single block. Scalpel away excess layers of paper beneath the block to minimize paper bulk. Adjust the position using a cocktail stick, since the pieces are very small and fiddly to handle. Build up the remaining eight blocks in the same way. Do not worry if the gaps between pieces are not identical.

Day Two

Step 9

Apply one coat of diluted PVA to the entire tile, followed by several coats of varnish. Allow the manufacturer's recommended drying time between coats.

8

9

Sorting the tesserae

For ease of working sort the tiny card tesserae into envelopes according to their individual sizes. Cut the pieces out during weekends and evenings prior to making the project to save time.

Gilded window recess

This evocative 'gilded' tile treatment is both pretty and practical, and very easy to achieve. It is best reserved for areas not in constant contact with water.

Window recesses offer the perfect opportunity to indulge in quite dramatic decorating effects that might be overwhelming if used more liberally. As this is an area usually overlooked by even the most fervent decorator, making a feature of your window recess is guaranteed to induce gasps of admiration from all who see it. Even more satisfying is watching people's faces as you reveal the humble beginnings of this beautiful design. They will never believe that such a rich, multilayered effect started life as plain, reject tiles.

Lettering in all its forms is very versatile as a decorative motif. You can, of course, use old deeds and letters if you are lucky enough to have some, and photocopy them to achieve similar effects, but in order to make this project truly achievable in a weekend we have supplied a page of copperplate Latin script and devised an alphabet on page 76 ready for photocopying.

Metal leaf is now widely available in craft shops and by mail order, and gilding of this random nature is satisfyingly simple. Children enjoy flicking the coffee granules onto the tiles and do so in a more relaxed, sporadic way than adults ever will. If you cannot borrow a small child, loosen up as best you can and enjoy the thrill of legitimately flinging coffee at the walls! Like most decorative effects, the result looks dreadful while in action, but suddenly wonderful on completion.

Planning your time

DAY ONE
AM: Plan tiling; cut tiles to fit. Tile recess and leave to set

PM: Photocopy alphabet and script; cut out blocks of text to cover tiles; cut out individual words and letters

DAY TWO
AM: Grout tiles and clean

PM: Apply text to cover each tile; age with coffee and tea; apply metal leaf and individual words and letters. Varnish

Tools and materials

Metal leaf

Acrylic gold size

Paintbrush

Nail scissors

Scalpel and cutting mat (optional)

Instant coffee granules

Tea bags

Shellac or acrylic varnish

Reject tiles, any colour

Templates on page 76

Buff-coloured powdered grout

Universal stainers in ochre and burnt umber

Clean rags or kitchen paper

Large scissors

PVA adhesive

Scuffing tool

Notched tile adhesive spreader

Tile spacers

Glass cleaner

Disposable gloves

Tile squeegee

Tracing paper

Soft pencil

Masking tape

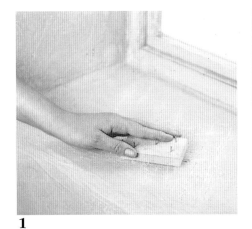

1

Day One

Step 1

Scuff the surface of the window recess with the scuffing tool to provide a key for the tile adhesive. Seal with PVA adhesive diluted in a ratio of approximately 50:50 with water.

Step 2

Roughly try out the tile spacing to ascertain whether any cuts are necessary to fit them properly. On the horizontal surface, place tiles from the centre of the sill outwards. Spread tile adhesive onto the horizontal surface of the recess. Use the notched spreader to achieve a uniform thickness of adhesive. Apply the tiles.

Step 3

Apply the tiles to the vertical surfaces of the recess. Start at the bottom and work upwards, making any cuts necessary at the top of the recess. Use tile spacers between each one to keep them evenly spaced as the adhesive sets.

2

3

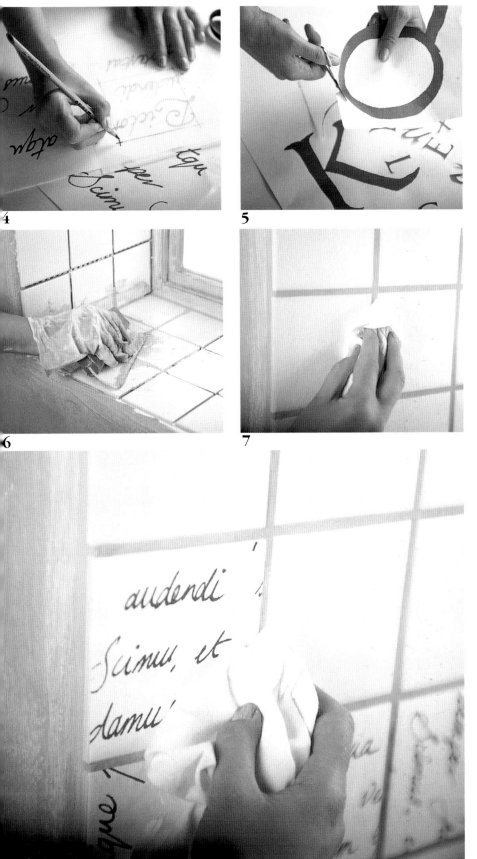

Step 4

Mark out the size of the tile onto tracing paper. Photocopy the Templates on page 76 to the required sizes. Place the tracing of the tile size over a sheet of text to ascertain a pleasing placement of the lettering within the tile. Transfer the corner marks onto the sheet of text and cut out with scissors or scalpel. Repeat until you have sufficient precut sheets to cover all the tiles.

Step 5

Cut individual letters from the alphabet and enlarged words from script photocopies using nail scissors and/or a scalpel.

Day Two

Step 6

Mix PVA adhesive with water, approximately 1 part PVA to 5 parts water, and colour this mixture with ochre and burnt umber universal stainers. Use this water to make up the powder grout to a dryish, mud-pie consistency. Apply with a tile squeegee and remove excess with a dry rag or kitchen paper.

Step 7

Thoroughly clean tiles using glass cleaner and kitchen paper for a lint-free result.

Step 8

Using PVA adhesive diluted with water in a ratio of roughly 1:1, apply to tiles and affix sheets of script. Run text alternately vertically and horizontally (reading left to right) to achieve a richly textured, random look.

9

Step 9

Make a strong cup of tea (three tea bags in a mug produces a good dyeing brew). Allow to cool before brushing all over the script-covered tiles. Allow to drip onto the grout to age. Add more tea randomly and allow to pool to form an attractive antiqued look.

Step 10

Roughly grind instant coffee granules in a mortar and pestle or in a plastic bag with a rolling pin, until some forms powder and some forms slightly smaller granules. Mask off surrounding areas and fling coffee randomly over the tiles for an age-spotted effect.

Step 11

Apply acrylic gold size randomly to the tiles using a small paintbrush. Leave for approximately 15 minutes or until clear and tacky, rather than opaque and wet.

Using different colours

This project would look completely different using silver coloured leaf (aluminium). Photocopy the text in black and white to produce a dark grey colour, and instead of tea dyeing, colour the script with dilute blue ink. Exchange the coffee splattering for ink splattered from an old toothbrush. Mask off the surrounding area!

10

11

12

13

14

Step 12

Press a sheet of metal (gold-coloured) leaf against each tile using a gentle pressing movement through a piece of kitchen paper so as not to tear the fragile metal. Leave to set for a few minutes before brushing away excess with a dry paintbrush. Burnish with a soft rag.

Step 13

Using the 1:1 PVA dilution, apply letters and words randomly across all the tiles. A particularly attractive, hand-made look occurs where words and letters flow across two or more tiles. Cut out that part of the letter that would cross in the grout line and discard. As with the blocks of text, the words will look more harmonious if placed reading from left to right as you look at the window.

Step 14

Varnish tiles with several coats of shellac for a pleasing rich golden tone, allowing each coat to dry thoroughly before applying the next. Try to keep varnish away from the grout as the contrast of the matt grout and the smooth sheen of the tiles is particularly appealing. For a speedier result simply brush over the entire surface.

Mosaic mirror frame

A modern classic in a restrained coffee and caramel palette, this simple-to-make frame includes mirrored tesserae and provides the perfect project for the novice mosaicist.

Planning your time

DAY ONE
AM: Mask off mirror; scuff and seal frame. Cut tesserae into quarters. Roughly plan design. Cut mirrored tesserae to fit inner and outer edges of frame

PM: Apply adhesive and tile to inner edge, outer edge, flat face of frame

DAY TWO
AM: Grout

Tools and materials

Mirror in flat profile frame

Masking tape

Mirrored square tesserae

Glass tesserae in caramel, copper, black and coffee shades

Scuffing tool

PVA adhesive

Paintbrush

Tile nippers

Goggles

Cocktail sticks

Wooden tongue depressors

Tile adhesive

Powdered grout (white)

Clean rags

Abrasive kitchen pads

Short-bristled, hard stencil brush

Disposable gloves

Patio cleaner (from tile shops) or dilute hydrochloric acid (from chemists)

When you visit a supplier of mosaic tiles, allow plenty of time. It is guaranteed that you will become quite overwhelmed by the vast array of colour and texture that greets you. Even the more experienced can still be rather bewildered when confronted with what seems at first like a never-ending amount of choices in colour and texture.

When you have settled down you will realize that most suppliers have duplicate tesserae in various formats. Loose tiles are often available, sometimes sold in bargain mixed bags, although you will then have to make do with the colours supplied, which may tend to be rather bright and not at all in keeping with the sophisticated feel intended for this project. Tiles are also sold in sheets of varying sizes, and by weight. The shop staff will be able to advise you on the most economical way to buy for the size of project you are planning.

This mirror frame is a satisfyingly fast-growing project, and can be made using just a few small sheets of glass tesserae and a bag of mirrored tesserae. Although you can change the colours to suit your own decorating scheme, it is recommended that you stick to a limited palette for the most professional, elegant results. Aim for a mirror that looks as if it has emerged from a chic designer store rather than from a penny bazaar.

1

Day One

Step 1
Mask off the mirror with masking tape.

Step 2
Scuff the frame with a scuffing tool to provide a good key for the adhesive.

Step 3
Seal the frame with PVA adhesive diluted approximately 50:50 with water. This provides an even better key for good adhesion and seals the frame against damp which could cause the mosaic to lift off.

2

3

Finding a frame

Most mosaic suppliers have a range of flat frames that are perfect for this project. Alternatively, use this method to jazz up a junk-shop find or a chain-store bargain.

4

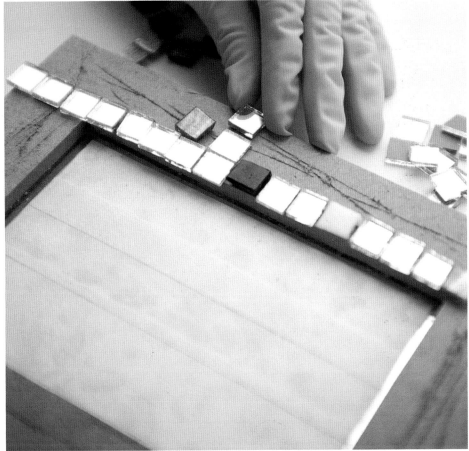

5

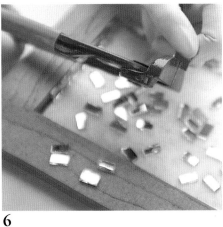

6

Step 4

Wearing goggles and gloves, cut the glass tesserae into halves, then into quarters with nippers. Place the curved side of the nippers towards the tile, just a tiny way across the tile. Exert equal pressure on the opposite side of the tile with your thumb and forefinger as you press the nippers together. The tile should break neatly in half, but do not worry if it does not; tesserae do not always break obligingly, even for the most skilled mosaicist.

Step 5

Experiment laying out the tesserae on the frame to ascertain whether further cuts are necessary, and to gauge the spacing between tiles.

Step 6

Cut the mirrored tesserae to fit in the area between the surface of the mirror and the flat face of the frame.

7

Step 7

Glue the cut mirrored tesserae to the inner edge of the frame with tile adhesive. Make sure you leave even gaps between tesserae.

Step 8

Cut, if cuts are necessary, further mirrored tesserae to place around the outer edge of the frame. Apply these to the outer edge.

Step 9

Apply mirrored and coloured tesserae onto the flat face of the frame in a random checkerboard pattern. In this direct method of mosaic the tesserae are applied with the ridged side down. The tiles should sit butted up against the tiles covering the inner and outer edges of the frame, but leaving enough room for grout beneath. The mirrored tiles are much thinner than the coloured glass tiles, so allow them to sit on the surface of the adhesive, but push the thicker tiles well down into it. This will give a smooth, flat surface. Take care to leave sufficient space for grout by removing any adhesive that creeps up around the tesserae. A cocktail stick is perfect for this fiddly, but necessary task. Allow to dry overnight.

8

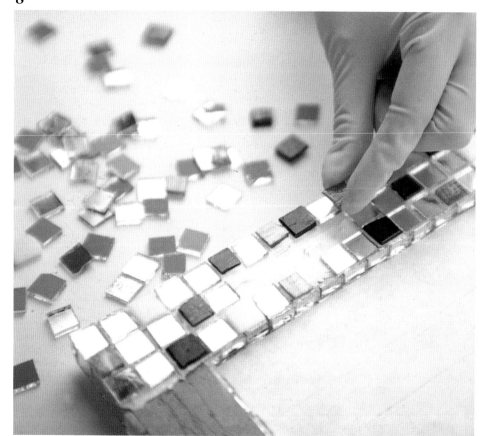

9

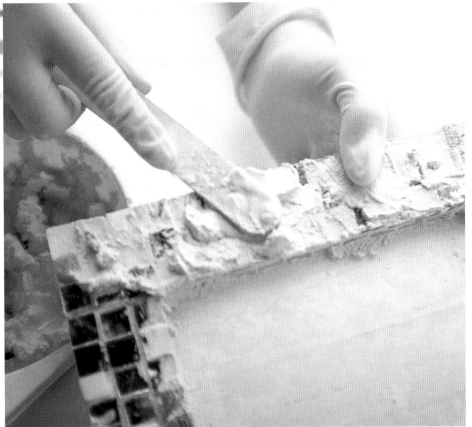

10

Day Two

Step 10

Mix up the grout using water that has PVA added in a ratio of approximately 1 part PVA to 5 parts water for greater adhesion to the frame. Make the grout fairly stiff and dry. Grout vertical, then horizontal surfaces, using a tongue depressor as a spreader. Work in all directions, pressing the grout well into all the gaps.

Step 11

Wearing gloves to protect your hands from any sharp, protruding tesserae, rub off excess grout with a dry rag. Remove any remaining grout with an abrasive pad and/or a stiff-bristled stencil brush. Give the mosaic a final clean a few days after completion using patio cleaner or dilute hydrochloric acid. Wear goggles and gloves, and wash off well with copious amounts of water before polishing with a soft cloth.

11

Making mirrored tesserae

Mirrored tesserae, although convenient, are comparatively expensive. You could make your own tesserae by cutting down a mirror tile with a glass cutter. Wear goggles and gloves to protect your eyes and hands against flying shards of glass.

Memorabilia china fountain

This whimsical fountain gives a new lease of life to broken china that you just cannot bear to throw away. It makes a stunning garden feature, with its perpetually pouring teapot.

Everyone has experienced the heart-sinking moment when a favourite piece of china jumps from your slippery hand onto the hard floor, emerging rather less intact than is useful. It feels almost unbearably brutal simply to discard the cherished item, particularly when the piece is largely complete save a hairline crack or chipped rim.

If you have been hoarding broken china for years, never knowing quite what to do with those treasured fragments of your family's history – your daughter's first plate, wedding china, a childhood cereal bowl – this charming fountain recycles them all to produce a uniquely personal folly on an attainable scale.

Children of all ages will enjoy picking out their favoured pieces from long ago, with the added appeal of the china being featured in a simple fountain. No-one will guess that such a richly decorative fountain started life as a cheap plastic wall planter and a sheet of wood, which makes the project doubly satisfying. Equally, you could mosaic over an existing fountain.

An inexpensive self-contained pump, the pipe fed through the spout of a beloved broken teapot, provides the water flow. A simple backing board of exterior-grade plywood is a sturdy weatherproof support, and the planter forms the splash pool. The diverse elements are unified by sticking to a limited colour range of rose pink, white and cobalt blue highlighted with gold. Planted tea cups add a contrast in texture and the planting can be changed seasonally. Drill holes in the cup bases if more drainage is needed. If you live in a cold climate make sure you use frost-proof tile adhesive.

A final clean with patio cleaner or dilute hydrochloric acid will make your mosaic fountain sparkle. Take care to rinse off well.

Planning your time

DAY ONE
AM: Mark and cut out plywood shape; screw bowl onto wood. Mark out key elements. Drill pipe holes; feed through water pipe and cable. Glue teapot and wide pipe

PM: Make mosaic

DAY TWO
AM: Grout

Tools and materials

19 mm (¾ in) exterior-grade plywood

Tape measure

Pencil and chalk

Abrasive kitchen pads

Hard, short-bristled stencil brush

Jigsaw or coping saw

Flat-backed plastic planter

Screws and screwdriver

Pump

Drill and 19 mm (¾ in) flat drill bit

1 m (3 ft) plastic pipe, diameter to match pump outlet size

20 cm (8 in) of 38 mm (1½ in) plastic waste pipe

Masking tape

Waterproof epoxy adhesive

Waterproof tile adhesive

Broken china (including cups, teapot, saucers)

Beads and buttons

Varnish

Paintbrush

Sealing mastic

Tile nippers

Hammer and sacking

Scuffing tool

Waterproof PVA adhesive

Day One

Step 1

Mark out half of the scroll-topped shape that forms the back board of the fountain onto tracing paper. Mark a central line down the length of the plywood piece, then trace the design onto one half of the plywood. Turn the tracing paper over and trace the same lines onto the other half to ensure a symmetrical design. Cut along the lines with an electric jigsaw or a coping saw.

Step 2

Screw a flat-backed plastic planter onto the plywood shape at the base to form the splash bowl.

Step 3

Scuff the surface of the wood using a scuffing tool to provide a good key for the tile adhesive.

Step 4

Seal the wood backboard and bowl with a coat of waterproof PVA diluted 50:50 with water.

Step 5

Roughly lay out the key elements of the design; for example, the teapot, whole plates, saucers etc. Chalk out the position of these elements on the board.

Assembling pieces of china

This project is quite labour intensive and involves vast quantities of china nibbled into tiny pieces to produce a really rich, textural result. As such, you may like to begin assembling your 'pool' of nibbled pieces during the evenings of the week prior to making the fountain. Mosaic is undoubtedly more relaxing when you have lots of pre-cut, pre-sorted pieces to choose from as you work.

1

2

3

4

5

6

Step 6

Using a 19 mm (³/₄ in) flat drill bit, drill a hole behind the teapot position to take the water pipe. Drill a second hole through the wood and bowl, above the water line and in one corner. This will take the water pipe and the electric cable.

Step 7

Place the pump in the splash bowl. Feed the water pipe leading from the pump through the lower hole in the backing board, from front to back; then up and through the upper hole, from back to front. The water pipe is now placed to feed into the teapot and through the spout.

Step 8

Fix a short length of wide pipe to the pool internally, to cover the second drilled hole. Use waterproof epoxy adhesive, securing with masking tape until the glue has set. This wider pipe allows you to feed the water pipe unobtrusively up and around the back of the board to allow the water to recirculate. The electric cable from the pump can also be fed through this pipe to conceal it. The wide pipe will be covered in mosaic to blend in with the rest of the fountain. The water pipe and electric cable can be fed back through this channel to remove the pump for annual cleaning and servicing.

7

8

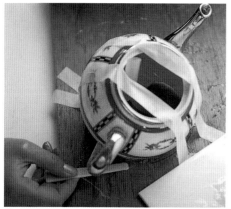

9

Step 9

Spread epoxy adhesive around the teapot area. Fix the teapot, angling the spout down and outwards towards the bowl of the fountain. Hold it with masking tape until the glue has set.

Step 10

Fix other key elements of the design such as pot lids and teacup halves using a thick bed of waterproof grey tile adhesive.

Step 11

Break up the remaining china into manageable fragments. Do this by using first a hammer, tapped against the china wrapped in sacking, then nippers. Wear gloves and goggles as protection.

Grinding the teapot spout

If your teapot has not broken at an obliging angle, you can cut it to fit by using an angle grinder, available from tool hire shops. Wear ear defenders, goggles and gloves when using. An angle grinder will also cut cups neatly in half. It is possible to nip and sand china to size without recourse to this power tool, but performing this task by hand is infinitely slower and results in a greater number of undesirable breakages.

10

11

12

14

13

Step 12

Build up the mosaic by working one small area at a time. Work symmetrically to achieve good visual balance; for example, if applying blue china to one side of the scroll top, build up the other side simultaneously. Cover the entire fountain in mosaic, using beads, buttons – anything that is pretty and has significance for you. Protect any vulnerable items with varnish.

Day Two

Step 13

Mix frost-proof grey powder grout with water to which waterproof PVA has been added in a ratio of approximately 1 part PVA to 5 parts water. Aim for a dryish mud-pie consistency. Wearing gloves, work the grout well into every crack and crevice of the design. Remove excess with dry rags, abrasive kitchen pads and a hard stencil brush.

Step 14

Screw a small piece of 50 x 25 mm (2 x 1 in) softwood to the back of the fountain at the top; screw a D ring onto this. Fix a further piece of 50 x 25 mm (2 x 1 in) softwood to the bottom of the panel, behind the splashpool; this will provide a spacer so that the water pipe that runs up behind the fountain does not become squashed.

Daisy mosaic table

This design of daisies created from broken, reject tiles transforms a dilapidated junk shop table into an attractive and useful piece of garden furniture.

This table base with its faded green paint was found languishing outside a junk shop. The top had completely disintegrated long ago and the base itself was somewhat unstable, but the delicate proportions and gentle colour were perfect. Even the rust spots were evocative of summers past.

Hammered into shape, the wobbly nature of the base improved considerably, but it was necessary to have a new top cut from exterior-grade plywood. Smaller, independent timber yards are usually happy to supply a custom cutting service for a small price. If you are mosaicing an existing table top, scuff and seal first of all.

The very cheapest, machine-made tiles are perfect for mosaic as they are thin and you can cut them with blissful ease. Those used here are seconds from a factory shop. The pieces are relatively large to give the design a strong, graphic look, so the work grows with satisfying speed. Take care with all mosaic work to consider the grout lines as elements that are of equal importance to the mosaic pieces themselves. Leave gaps of equal width so that there is a pleasing flow between pieces to produce a cohesive end result rather than the effect of an ill-fitting jigsaw. Remember, when choosing your tiles, that the green colour for the stems needs to be of a dramatically darker tone than that used in the background, or the trailing stem and leaf design will simply be lost in the ground colour. The background was produced from a mixture of toning shades for a softly textured look, but you could stick to just one colour for a more striking contrast. If you live in a cold climate and the table is going to be left outdoors, make sure you use frost-proof grout and adhesive.

Planning your time

DAY ONE
AM: Scuff and seal table top; mark out design. Prepare pieces of tile for daisies, leaves, stems and table edge; apply flower motifs, leaves and stem.

PM: Smash and nip tiles for background; apply background and edging tiles

DAY TWO
AM: Grout

Tools and materials

Table base and top

New table top (if necessary) cut from exterior-grade plywood

Waterproof PVA adhesive

Scuffing tool

Hammer and sacking

Paintbrush

Chalk

Clean rags

Goggles

Reject, machine-made tiles (ivory, yellow, dark green, beige, aqua and pale green)

Tile nippers

Tile cutter

Sanding block

Powdered frost-proof grout (grey)

Frost-proof, waterproof powder tile adhesive (grey) (for example, swimming pool tile adhesive)

Wooden tongue depressors

Disposable gloves

Patio cleaner (from tile shops) or dilute hydrochloric acid (from chemists)

Short-bristled hard stencil brush

Day One

Step 1
Scuff the surface of the table using a scuffing tool.

Step 2
Brush on a 50:50 mix of waterproof PVA adhesive and water to seal the wood against moisture. Leave to dry.

Step 3
Draw on the design very roughly using chalk. All you need are circles to represent the positions of the daisies and single lines to represent the stems. Follow the Templates on page 77 to help you with the design.

Step 4
Wearing goggles and gloves, place the ivory, dark green, and yellow tiles individually between layers of sacking, then smash each one centrally with a hammer. Open the sacking to check how the tile has broken. If necessary, fold the sacking back over the tile and hit with the hammer again until you have several large triangular pieces.

Step 5
Still wearing goggles and gloves, use tile nippers to nibble the shards of yellow tile into approximate circles for the daisy centres. Nip some in half to form semi circles, so that some daisies span the edge of the table. This gives a fresh, spontaneous feel to the design, as if the daisy chain is truly scattered across the surface of the table.

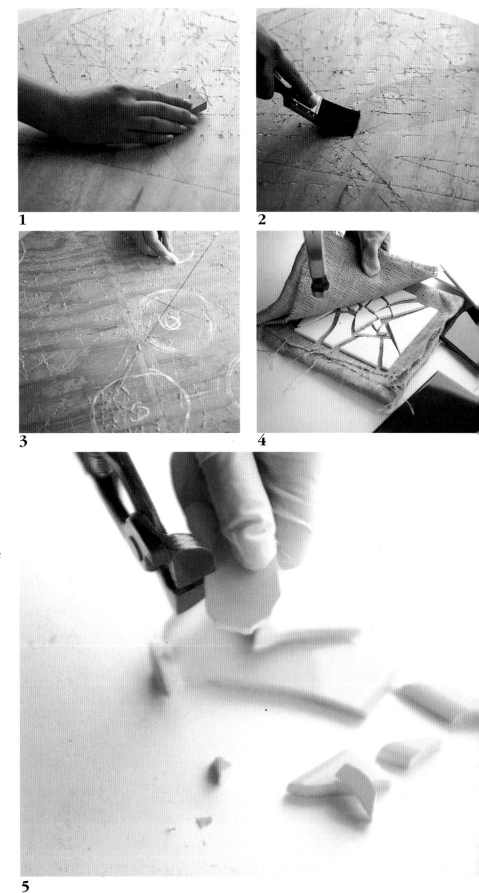

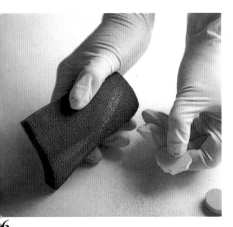

6

Step 6

Sand the daisy centres with a sanding block to remove jagged edges, but allow them to remain not quite round. Calculated imperfection is a distinctive element of the finished design; perfect circles would look ill at ease with the graphic petals.

Step 7

Some of the larger triangular pieces of dark green and ivory tile may need slight nipping to produce appropriately sized pieces to represent the petals and leaf shapes. Again, do not try to produce realistic petal shapes. Keep the shapes starkly angular.

Step 8

'Butter' each tessera on the reverse with tile adhesive, using a wooden tongue depressor or spatula. Then apply the flower centres and petals to the table, loosely following the chalk marks. Do not try to keep strictly within the chalked circles or the design will look too forced. Aim for a feeling of spontaneity, using the tile pieces almost as they come to hand rather than worrying about finding the perfectly shaped petal.

7

8

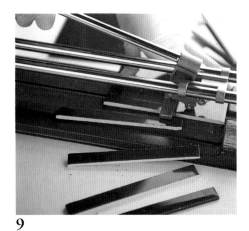

9

Step 9

Cut strips of dark green tile on the tile cutter to form the stems. The required width will depend on the scale of your design. These strips are approximately 1.5 cm (3/4 in) wide, making a good visual balance to the flower heads, which are around 20 cm (8 in) across. From the four outside edges of a tile only, cut strips from your chosen background colour the thickness of the table top, plus a tile thickness – these will be used for the mosaic band placed around the edge of the table.

Step 10

Nip the resulting long strips into smaller pieces. The edging pieces look neatest cut into squares, while the stems look best cut into random lengths.

Step 11

'Butter' and apply the stems and leaves as you applied the flowers.

10

11

12

13

14

Step 12

Create a 'pool' of randomly mixed background colour by smashing, then nipping, beige, pale green and aqua tiles into pieces approximately 1.5 cm (³/4 in) square. Do not aim for perfect regularity in the shapes produced.

Step 13

'Butter' and apply the background pieces, taking care to preserve even grout spacing.

Step 14

'Butter' and apply the edge pieces, taking care to line up the glazed edge of the tile with the surface of the table for a smooth finish.

Day Two

Step 15

Mix up the powder grout, incorporating waterproof PVA adhesive in a ratio of approximately 1 part PVA to 5 parts water before you mix. This gives the grout increased adhesion to the wooden table top. Mix the grout to a dryish, mud-pie consistency and press well into the gaps between the tiles. Because the tiles are not necessarily of uniform thickness, you may find it easier to grout with your fingers (protected by gloves) rather than a squeegee. Rub away any excess grout with a clean, dry rag and abrasive kitchen pads. A hard, short-bristled stencil brush is also useful for removing grout from the corners of mosaic pieces. A few days after completion, clean the mosaic with patio cleaner or dilute hydrochloric acid. Wear goggles and gloves and wash off the solution with plenty of water.

15

Safety advice

Remember that the edges of glazed smashed or nipped tiles are essentially broken glass. Wear gloves when working with broken tiles and handle all the pieces carefully.

'Antique' tiled fireplace

Here, tiles painted in an 'antique' style decorate a fireplace. The classic-looking top could also be applied to an area above a shelf or cupboard for a formal look.

Who can resist buying tiles from factory shops and flea markets! However, you usually find that they sit around being used as makeshift pot stands and trivets while awaiting a project more worthy of their beauty. These charming Delft-style tiles were a case in point.

In this project plain tiles and inexpensive rejects give a striking change of scale and eke out a meagre initial supply of Delft tiles. Hand painted with ceramic paints to mimic old tiles, they integrate perfectly with the pretty floral motifs. You may strike lucky and find large hand-painted tiles in a junk shop, but it is much more satisfying to paint your own. Also, you can be sure of having two end tiles of exactly the same size, and at a considerably reduced cost than their antiquated equivalent.

Although the tiles in this project have been used to dress up a fireplace, you could also run a decorative border of tiles around a room, or highlight a small area of a room, such as a window or door, by adding a mix and match border of junk shop and reject shop tiles and your own hand-painted ones.

The formal 'pediment', which gives such a smart, classical look, is simply assembled from cheap DIY chain-store mouldings and two plate shelves. Do not be put off by the technical-looking mitre saw used here. It makes light work of the project and is simple to use.

Day One

Step 1
Clean and condition a large tile with proprietary cleaner compatible with ceramic paints. These are usually sold as part of the same range. The conditioner provides a good key for the paint. Follow the manufacturer's directions precisely to ensure even adhesion.

Step 2
Using tracing paper and a soft pencil, transfer the design from the Template on page 78 onto the tile. To achieve a more handmade effect, make some of the lines more uneven than others.

Step 3
Paint the design onto the tile with an art brush. Repeat the conditioning, transferring and painting on another large tile. Follow the manufacturer's directions for setting the paint hard. Many ceramic paints are cold setting, but some need to be fired in a domestic oven to fix. Varnish and 'antique' when set by adding a two-part crackle glaze following the manufacturer's instructions. Accentuate the crackles by rubbing dark oil paints into them. 'Antique' the new Delft-style tiles to match in similar fashion.

Step 4
Roughly lay out the tiles above the fireplace to assess the final spacing and best placement of the motifs. Mark out just inside the area to be tiled to give a guide for adhesive application.

Step 5
Using a scuffing tool, roughen the surface of the wall. Seal with PVA adhesive diluted approximately 50:50 with water to ensure reliable adhesion.

1

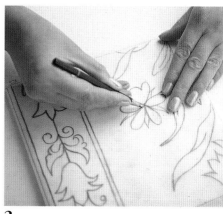

2

3

4

5

6

7

8

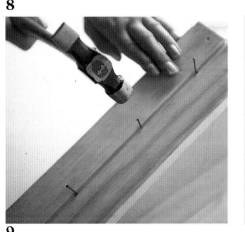

9

Step 6

Using a notched spreader, spread tile adhesive onto the wall approximately 3 mm (1/8 in) deep. Apply tiles, using a twisting movement on each tile to embed it squarely and firmly. Leave to dry for several hours or overnight.

Day Two

Step 7

Mix PVA adhesive with water in a ratio of approximately 1 part PVA to 5 parts water and colour this mixture with ochre and burnt umber universal stainers. Use this water to make up the powder grout to a dryish, mud-pie consistency. Apply carefully with a brush and remove the excess grout gently with a soft rag.

Step 8

Using a mitre saw, cut the plate shelves to the desired angle for the pediment, remembering that the angles in a triangle total 180 degrees. Cut to length and panel pin them to form a triangle, making sure that the plate groove is on the outside of the triangle. Place this on the MDF. Draw around inside the triangle and cut the MDF to size using a regular saw.

Step 9

Place the MDF triangle inside the triangle border until it is level with the plate groove. Panel pin the two together. Using a glue gun, put dowel in place to conceal the plate groove and provide texture. Mitre cut ogee moulding and, using the glue gun, fix it onto the MDF triangle for a classical look. Fix to the wall with coving adhesive and paint with ivory eggshell paint.

Further decorative ideas for tiles

You could even use pressed flowers in a design like this, which will not need to withstand frequent contact with water. Simply protect with two or more coats of clear spray varnish. Forget-me-nots at the corners of a tile would give a charming *trompe l'oeil* Delft-like effect.

Glossary

Mitre saw

Mastic frame

Abrasive kitchen pads
Used to remove excess grout from virtually flat mosaic surfaces.

Acrylic gold size
Glue to affix metal leaf.

Ceramic paint
Available from craft shops in a myriad of colours in either cold set or heat set variants. Both types will set hard on ceramic tiles if properly prepared according to the paint manufacturer's instructions. Ceramic paint is perfect for small areas of tile painting; in particular, highly decorative designs.

Cleaner/conditioner
Proprietary product sold alongside small pots of ceramic paint to provide a clear, secure key for good adhesion.

Cocktail sticks
Small wooden sticks useful for placing fiddly pieces of mosaic.

Cotton buds
Indispensable for cleaning fiddly areas or removing paint splashes; also for placing fiddly pieces of mosaic without pushing too deeply into the adhesive bed.

Disposable gloves
Useful for grouting and other messy aspects of tiling and mosaic work.

Dowelling
Round-sectioned timber, usually made of ramin or pine.

Expandable sponge
Compressed sponge that is easy to draw a design on when dry, but which expands to form a painting stamp when placed in water for a few seconds.

Hydrochloric acid
Acid used for cleaning cement scum from the face of a finished mosaic. It is sold pre-diluted in chemists. Always wear goggles and gloves when using and rinse the mosaic liberally with fresh water after use.

Mastic frame
This is used for applying certain glues and sealants accurately and evenly, for example EVA adhesive.

Medium density fibreboard (MDF)
Smooth board made of glue and sawdust. Ask for the formaldehyde-free type.

Metal leaf
Thin sheets of metal used in gilding.

Mitre saw
Saw with selectable fixed angles and support to cut mitred joints accurately and simply.

Notched adhesive spreader
Spreader that makes it simple to apply a uniformly thick bed of adhesive, so ensuring perfectly flat tiling.

Notched spreader

Powder grout
Cement-based dry powder that when mixed with water produces a strong, matt grout. Also available in a frost-proof formula.

Protective goggles and dust mask
Essential when nipping tiles.

PVA (Polyvinyl acetate adhesive)
A white water-based glue that gives a strong bond. Watered down it can be used as a sealant. When dry it gives a clear finish. Also available in a waterproof version that is an alternative to EVA.

Quilt tape
Narrow masking tape from quilt suppliers, perfect for masking off grout while painting tiles.

Scalpel
Extremely sharp knife used for precision cutting.

Scuffing tool
Home-made tool comprising panel pins driven through a piece of scrap wood. Used to deliberately roughen surfaces to provide a key for tile adhesive.

Shellac
Golden-coloured varnish used to seal metal leaf to prevent it from tarnishing.

Smalti
Hand-made mosaic pieces of irregular size and texture.

Stencil brush
Short-bristled stiff brush used in this book for specific cleaning of fiddly areas in mosaic projects after grouting, particularly those involving awkwardly shaped objects.

Tesserae
Generic term used to describe individual component of a mosaic; literally – tile.

Tile nippers
Spring-loaded pincers for trimming tiles and china to size.

Tile saw
Carbide-bladed saw for cutting awkward shapes in tiles and china.

Tile squeegee
Soft rubber-bladed tool perfect for spreading and cleaning grout on smooth, flat surfaces.

Tongue depressors
Inexpensive wooden spatulas available from chemists. Useful, flexible, perfectly clean and smooth disposable spreaders for both tile adhesive and grout.

Universal stainers
Inexpensive colours that may be used to custom-tint many kinds of paint, as well as the water used to mix up powdered grout.

Waterproof tile adhesive
Adhesive suitable for projects requiring frequent contact or total immersion in water.

Tile squeegee

Tongue depressors

Tile cutters

Templates

Gilded window recess

A B C D
E F G H
I J K L
M N O P
Q R S T
U V W X
Y Z

Pictoribus atque poetis. Quidibet audendi semper fuit aequa potestas. Scimus, et hanc veniam petimusque damasque vicissim Pictoribus atque poetis. Quidibet audendi semper fuit aequa potestas. Scimus, et hanc veniam petimusque damusque vicissim. Pictoribus atque poetis. Quidibet audendi semper fuit aequa potestas. Scimus, et hanc veniam petimusque damusque vicissim

Templates

Daisy mosaic table

Templates

'Antique' tiled fireplace

Dark brown

Dark blue

Dark brown

Golden yellow

Dark green

Dark brown

Pink

Dark brown

These colours are suggestions only. Use your own ideas and outline shapes with other colours.

Golden yellow

Light green

Dark green

Light green

Pink with blue edging

Dark brown

Golden yellow

Dark green

Pink

Golden yellow

Light green

Suppliers

The Kitchen Range
Hillier's Yard
High Street
Marlborough
Wiltshire
SN8 1BE
Tel. 01672 514588
*Green recycled glass tumbler
in Daisy mosaic table project
page 64.*

**The Merchants House Trust
Shop**
132 High Street
Marlborough
Wiltshire
SN8 1HN
Tel. 01672 511491
*Gold plaster candle base and
church candle in Gilded window
recess project page 46.*

Patios and Ponds of Hungerford
4a Bath Road
Hungerford
Berkshire
RG17 0HE
Tel. 01488 686140
*Pre-graded pebbles in Pebble
mosaic floor project page 12.*

H. and R. Johnson Tiles
Highgate Tile Works
Tunstall
Stoke on Trent
ST6 4JX
Tel. 01782 575575
*An encylopaedic range. Prismatics
machine-made tiles in Gingham
bath panel project page 22 and
Daisy mosaic table project
page 64.*

Marlborough Tiles Factory Shop
16 High Street
Marlborough
Wiltshire
SN8 1AA
Tel. 01672 515287
*Terracotta floor tiles in Pebble
mosaic floor project page 12, Delft
tiles, ivory barley twist and large
plain ivory tiles in 'Antique' tiled
fireplace project page 70, large tiles
and curved dado tiles in Painted
fabric tiles project page 16,
snowflake white (mottled) tiles
in Gilded window recess project
page 46.*

Ian Mankin
108 Regents Park Road
London NW1 8UR
Tel. 0171 722 0997
*Checked fabric on screen in
Gingham bath panel project
page 22.*

Newbury Bathrooms
28a Pound Street
Newbury
Berkshire
RG14 6EE
Tel. 01635 37810
*Bath in Gingham bath panel
project page 22.*

Specialist Crafts Direct
PO Box 247
Leicester LE1 9QS
Tel. 0116 2510405
*Acrylic gold size, brass metal leaf
and shellac for Gilded window
recess project page 46. Mail order
available.*

J. and M. Davidson
62 Ledbury Road
London W11 2AJ
Tel. 0171 243 2089
*Toiletries and towels in Gingham
bath panel project page 22.*

Walcot Reclamation
108 Walcot Street
Bath
Avon
BA1 5BG
Tel. 01225 444404
*Fireplace in 'Antique' tiled fireplace
project page 70, basin and taps in
Playing card splashback project
page 42, sink and taps in
Mediterranean colourwashed tiles
project page 8, basin and taps
in Découpage floral tiles project
page 30.*

Jardinerie
Finebush Garden Centre
Hay Lane
Wroughton
Swindon
Wiltshire
SN4 9QT
Tel. 01793 852736
*Metal chair in Daisy mosaic table
project page 64.*

Scumble Goosie
Lewiston Mill
Toadsmoor Road
Stroud
Gloucestershire
GL5 2TB
Tel. 01453 731305
*MDF screen in Gingham bath
panel project page 22.*

Index